MATT DAMON

A SHORT UNAUTHORIZED BIOGRAPHY

FAMELIFE BIOS

1

Who Is Matt Damon

Matthew Paige Damon, more commonly known as Matt Damon, is an award-winning American actor, producer, and screenwriter. He is well-known for his role in Jason Bourne films, the blockbuster film *The Martian* with a Golden Globe Award, and many more. Damon first sparked interest in acting at an early age, where he began his career as a teen in local community theaters. His first casting was for a commercial for TJ Maxx, and he said that he used the money he got from that commercial to take the train and meet up with an agent, which then paved the way for a part in the 1990 film *The Rising Son*. Matt began to rise in fame when he co-wrote the 1997 American drama film *Good Will Hunting* with Ben Affleck. They bagged an Academy Award and a Golden Globe Award for best original screenplay for that film, and Matt was also nominated for best actor. He then turned to production when he founded *LivePlanet* in 2000: a multimedia company started by Matt Damon, Ben Affleck, Chris

Moore, and Sean Bailey, through which they made the documentary series *Project Greenlight* which was nominated for an Emmy Award. Since then, Matt has been given various awards and nominations and was ranked third in the world's highest-paid actors in 2016 by Forbes with a whopping 55 million dollars income in that year alone.

On October 8, 1970, Matt Damon was born in Cambridge, Massachusetts but later moved to Newton for two years. His father was a stockbroker, and his mother used to teach in early childhood education. Matt and his older brother moved back to Cambridge in a six-family communal house with their mother after their parents separated when Matt was only two years old.

Damon found his passion for acting and started participating in local theater plays in Cambridge Rindge & Latin School. He landed his first big-screen appearance in the 198 films Mystic Pizza. He enrolled in Harvard but later on dropped out before graduating to play a role in Geronimo: An American Legend (1993). After being cast in several positions, Matt finally earned his well-deserved spotlight when Good Will Hunting (1997), a film he and Ben Affleck wrote and starred in, received various nominations and awards. Matt continued his success when he starred in The Talented Mr. Ripley (1999) and was named by the media as one of Hollywood's golden boys. In the 2000s, Damon started casting in action films like the Bourne Series, which gained him a lot of positive feedback and became one of his highest-grossing films to star in. He also plunged into Comedy movies when he starred in the comedy film Stuck On You (2003). In 2007, Matt starred again in two of his grossing film, Ocean's Thirteen and The Bourne Ultimatum. The Martian was released in 2015, where he won as best actor. Besides being an actor, he also became a producer and co-founded LivePlanet with his friends in 1998.

Matt Damon is a very successful celebrity. His talent earned him many awards and nominations, including an Academy Award and two Golden Globe Awards. He is also a screenwriter, which paved the way to his success. Matt is a co-founder of the production company Live Planet which produced several films and shows like Project Greenlight, Manchester by The Sea, and Promised Land. He did not forget to give back throughout his accomplishments and endeavors and started his organization like water.org to help people in need. Probably one of Matt's most significant and proudest achievements is being a father to 4 lovely daughters and raising them well.

2

Things People Have Said About Matt Damon

Matt Damon has garnered multiple nominations, awards, and even criticisms throughout his career. Up to this day, he is part of the Top 40 Highest Paid Actors of All Time with a net worth of over 160 million dollars. In 2007, he became the 2,343rd personality to be given a star on the Hollywood Walk of Fame and was also chosen as the "Sexiest Man Alive" by People Magazine. It started as a harmless prank by George Clooney when he paid for a full-page ad campaign with an embarrassing photo of Damon in a green Speedo from the movie Talented Mr. Ripley and said, "For your consideration, Sexiest Man Alive" and kept it going for around two years until Damon was finally chosen as The Sexiest Man Alive in 2007. Matt then got involved and received backlash from comments he made about sexual assault in Hollywood, where he was criticized as "tone deaf" after saying that people should focus more on men who are not sexual predators and that there is a difference between rape and simply patting someone on the butt. He says that this issue paved the way for a "culture of outrage," He then apologized for saying he wished he'd listen more before weighing in on the subject.

Some people questioned Damon's title as the sexiest man alive in 2007 since it all started building up because of a prank. He was the 22nd man awarded the label next to his friend Clooney, who started the joke. People Magazine, later on, killed the rumors and said, "George Clooney and Brad Pitt have shamelessly campaigned for him since 2001, but all it takes is one look at Damon's piercing blue eyes, crooked smile, and family-guy demeanor to understand why he has been chosen," in an interview. Although Damon was hesitant to accept the award, he said that they "gave an aging dad the ego boost of a lifetime." And that his stepdaughter thinks he's calmer now.

3

Matt Damon Is Born

Born in Cambridge, Massachusetts, on October 8, 1970, Matt Damon is the second son of Kent Damon and Nancy Paige. Matt has a brother, Kyle Damon, three years older than him and is a sculptor and artist. Matt recalled that he didn't have great privileges growing up, and he didn't ask for anything. They moved to Newton, and after two years, their parents divorced. Matt and his brother moved back to Cambridge with their mother and lived in a humble communal house where he met his longtime best friend, Ben Affleck, as his neighbor. They met when Matt was ten and Ben was eight years old. They shared their love for baseball as they are both Boston Red Sox fans. They also bonded with their passion for acting and started tag-teaming auditions.

Matt's mother, Nancy Carlsson-Paige, has been a professor at Lesley University for 30 years and founded the University's Center for Peaceable Schools. She spent her childhood in a small town outside Albany, New York, and loved playing outdoors. Her last name was the original "Pajari" before being changed to Paige. She is now known to be a creative author and a speaker about the effects of violence on children. She is also an advocate for education policies that promote social justice. Numerous awards have been given to her, including the Peace Educator of the Year, the Outstanding Educator Award, and a lifetime achievement award by the American Academy of Education Arts & Sciences in 2013. She also published six books primarily written to advocate children's well-being and encourage peace. She said she always knew Matt would be an actor, and Kyle would be an artist because she could see it in the way they played.

The father of Matt was Kent Telfer Damon (1942-2017), born in Springfield, Massachusetts, who was married to Celeste Kent and Nancy Paige. He worked as a financial Advisor for ten years at Paine Webber and eventually became the Vice President of the company. Kent co-founded Beacon Hill Capital in 1986, which is an investment firm for affordable housing. Before these jobs, Kent was a janitor at Harvard, which became the inspiration of Matt in writing the film Good Will Hunting. He also loved sports and outdoor activities and spent Sundays playing basketball, football, or baseball with his sons. He also developed his love for sailing and cruised for 30 years in the New England Shores. After his retirement, his newfound hobby was golf at Andover Country Club. He was then diagnosed with a rare type of cancer in 2011 and died after six years of battle with cancer at age 74.

Matthew's ancestry is English, Scottish, Finnish and Swedish descent. They came from a middle-class family of a stockbroker and professor and spent two years in Newton before his parents divorced. Matt said that being a middle-class child is tremendous wealth compared to the rest of the world.

4

Growing Up With Matt Damon

Matt grew up in two loving households even though his parents separated when he was just a toddler. He said that he never felt the need to lie to his parents. When he was around 15-17 years old, they would go backpacking across Mexico and Guatemala and enroll in a language school course where they would go to school for six hours and come home to a Mexican family where the only language is spoken in Spanish. After a few weeks, they are ready to travel across the country in a bus stuffed with chickens. Matt said that taking the trip opened his eyes to poverty not typically seen in Boston.

Matt Damon first went to Cambridge Alternative Public School (CAPS), now known as Graham and Parks, which has gained praise nationwide. In 1981, CAPS and a small neighborhood school, Webster School, joined to form Graham and Parks School. The school moved to a different street in 2003.

Matt studied high school in Cambridge Rindge and Latin School, a public high school with prominent alumni such as the poet E.E. Cunnings, actors Ben and Casey Affleck, composer Leroy Anderson, and many more. Matt was a great student in Cambridge Rindge and developed his love for acting as he began casting in school productions. He took drama classes and worked with Ben Affleck in High School Productions.

Matt attended Harvard University from 1988-to 1992, where he took a Bachelor of Arts and Majored in English. He first resided in Matthews Hall then moved to Lowell House. He was also a member of one of Harvard's most recognized social organizations, Delphic Club, which used to be an all-male club until 2017. He also wrote an early treatment of their award-winning screenplay Good Will Hunting in Harvard to submit an exercise for one of his English classes. Damon's passion for acting grew as he appeared in student theater plays like Burn This and made his on-screen film debut at 18 with a single-liner in the Romantic Comedy film *Mystic Pizza* (1988). He was then given a role in the 1990 film Rising Son and dropped out of college with just 12 credits remaining to graduate. He left Harvard to take a lead role in *Geronimo: an American Legend* (1993) in Los Angeles and a role in *School Ties* (1992).

2009
NALE
RAFICA

5

Matt Damon's Personal Relationships

The first rumored girlfriend of Matt was Skylar Statenstein during the late 1980s, and then he starred in the film Good Will Hunting (1997), where he met Minnie Driver, his co-actress, in the shoot at some point in 1996. Minnie is an English-American actress who is also a singer-songwriter who reportedly dated Damon from 1996-to 1997, which helped their chemistry in the film. After winning awards for the 1997 film, Matt became a well-known Hollywood star. He appeared in an Oprah Winfrey interview in which he publicly announced that he is no longer in a relationship and broke up with Minnie in front of national television. He was soon seen with a new lover, Winona Ryder. The two were introduced by a good friend, Gwyneth Paltrow. It was rumored that they were secretly dating in 1997 while Matt was known to be with Minnie by the public. He and Winona made their relationship public after being seen together at the pre-Oscar party in 1998. Their relationship didn't last long, and they broke up in 2000. It is speculated that their breakup is because Damon wanted to be with a civilian and couldn't be with a celebrity.

Matt did not have any past marriages. He is still married to his longtime partner, Luciana Barroso. They have been married since 2005.

Damon met the Argentinean-born Luciana Barroso, a single mother at that time, at a bar in Miami while shooting the comedy film Stuck on You in 2003. Luciana worked as a bartender in that bar when Matt and his friends came. Soon fans became a bit aggressive, and Matt hid behind the bar to get away from fans and had the opportunity to chat with Luciana. Even though he was a known actor, Luciana made him work behind bars that night as a bartender, and she said she gained a lot of tips that night because of Damon. They started dating and tied the knot in 2005 and have kept their love alive ever since.

Matt takes pride in being a great dad to four beautiful daughters with Luciana – Gia, Stella, Isabella, and Alexia. Matt mentioned in the past that public relationships aren't for him. That's why he's fortunate to marry Luciana, a civilian, where they can keep their relationship relatively private and be a somehow ordinary parent to his four kids. He said being with Luciana makes him feel normal and at ease. When asked how they keep their relationship steady, Matt said they have a rule where they can't spend more than two weeks away.

6

The Rise of Matt Damon

Being starred in the 1990 movie Rising Son was a pivotal stage in Matt's career. It was so successful that he landed roles in School Ties (1992) and Geronimo: An American Legend (1993), which made him drop out of college. After three years, his most notable appearance was in the 1996 movie Courage Under Fire, where he played a soldier with drug addictions. After that, he got the leading role in the film The Rainmaker (1997). The highlight of his career was when he co-wrote and starred in the movie Good Will Hunting which rocketed his career status after receiving 9 Academy Award nominations in 1998, one of which is the best actor nomination for Matt. They also got a Golden Globe Award and two Screen Actors Guild Award nominations. Many roles came his way after the award-winning film he co-wrote and starred in. He was described by the press as one of Hollywood's Golden Boys when he impressed everybody with his destructive boy role in The Talented Mr. Ripley (1999). Damon said he didn't want to do the same parts repeatedly. That's why from drama films, he indulged in the world of action-adventure movies in the year 2002. He starred in Robert Ludlum's novel, The Bourne Series. The people significantly took his endeavor as the adaptation earned almost 122 million dollars in the first film on the Bourne Franchise. In 2009, he won his third Academy Award as Francois Pienaar in Invictus (2009).

Matt Damon climbed up the ladder to fame from performing at school plays to Hollywood. He is an actor, a voice-over artist, a writer, producer, and philanthropist. His career rocketed after the release of Good Will Hunting in 1997, in which he starred and co-wrote. He's starred in various high-grossing films and received tons of nominations and awards ever since.

7

Significant Career Milestones

Matt received his first Oscar, together with Ben Affleck, for the script of Good Will Hunting. The film did not only get any Oscars, but it also obtained nine Academy Award nominations – one of which is the best actor for Matt and a Golden Globes for best screenplay. Since then, Matt has been nominated numerous times for his roles by several award-giving bodies like Screen Actors Guild Award, Oscars, Golden Globe Award, Emmy, and many more. He won two Golden Globe Awards: one for Good Will Hunting as the best screenplay, and one for The Martian as best actor. He was also the favorite Male Action Star in People's Choice Award for his role in The Bourne Ultimatum. With all this fame and awards, Matt put himself to good use. He has always been an advocate of human rights and saving the earth. He has helped millions of people get clean water to drink through his organization. He wanted to use his prominence to make a difference in the world and help people since he started from the bottom. Matt said in an interview that he didn't want to become like other celebrities where they get involved in many things but don't connect deeply; he wanted to use his privilege to communicate with other people around the world and help them.

In Matt Damon's first award-winning film, Good Will Hunting, he made only 600,000 dollars even though he co-wrote and starred in that movie. That movie was his rise to stardom, and it was big money at that time, but compared to what he makes today, it is relatively small. He has starred in numerous high-grossing films in Hollywood and received tons of nominations and awards. One of the highest-grossing films that Matt starred in was The Bourne Ultimatum (2007) which earned over 227 million dollars. Next in line would be Ocean's Eleven (2001) with 183 million dollars and True Grit (2010) with 171 million dollars. The whole franchise of The Bourne Series was very successful. One of Damon's famous movies is The Martian (2015), where he received an Empire Award for Best Actor.

8

Matt Damon's Friends and Foes

When it comes to Matt's feuds, the most famous one is his dispute with Jimmy Kimmel, which is, although fake, still very entertaining. It all started after just a few seasons of Jimmy Kimmel Live when Jimmy jokingly ended the show one night by saying that they ran out of time for Matt Damon. Kimmel clarified that he only made that joke because he thinks his show was lame and wanted to crack a laugh out of his producers, which he successfully did, and he didn't mean to say Damon's name. He was just the first person that popped into his mind. He started using it as a running joke on the show and would pretend that Damon was always cut off. In 2006, Damon appeared on the front only to be cut off after a few seconds of appearance, "I knew you were going to f—king do it," he said as the credits started rolling. Damon then found a way to get back at Jimmy in 2007, where he teamed up with Jimmy's girlfriend at that time, Sarah Silverman, and made a music video claiming they slept together.

Jimmy, of course, fired back with a video starring Matt's best friend, Ben Affleck. Since then, the two had a fair share of sabotaging each other like, Matt kicking Jimmy out of the Handsome Men's Club, Jimmy sabotaging Matt on the Oscars, and many more. They even tried out couples counseling to settle their dispute, which ended badly. The feud still goes on when Jimmy was filming an episode of the show just recently in his house when suddenly, Matt came out of the room with Kimmel's wife in a robe. Although the feud is still ongoing, Matt and Jimmy sure are buddies in real life.

Ben Affleck played such a significant role in Matt Damon's life. The two became best friends when they were still 8 and 10 years old. Both educators introduced their mothers, and they lived just blocks away from each other in Massachusetts. They bonded over baseball and shared the same passion for acting and writing. They attended the same school where they tag-teamed in auditioning for roles in plays and films. Their first shared screen journey together was in the movie Fields of Dreams, where they appeared in crowd shots as baseball fans. The two started rising in fame when they wrote and starred in Good Will Hunting, in which they gathered numerous awards and nominations. Their friendship is cemented the moment Affleck defends Matt from a fight. Affleck tackled the guy off when a bigger man beat up Matt. Matt remembered that moment and said how good a friend Ben is for putting himself in the wrong position for Matt. They have been friends for decades and continued supporting each other as they did before, even financially when they used to have a joint account.

Since 2003, Damon's regular date to social events has been his wife, Luciana. One of Matt's most unforgettable Oscars events was in 2017 when Jimmy Kimmel hosted the event and brought his long-time feud with Matt on the stage of the Oscars. It started with a photo Jimmy posted on Instagram where he doodled on Matt's seat card with the caption "Best Picture Nominee Matt Damon" and then later on jokingly included in his speech his dismay about Matt's choice of roles wherein he handed over a significant role to his friend Casey Affleck just to partake in a Chinese ponytail movie instead. Damon clapped back with an attempt to trip Jimmy as he was walking towards the audience. When Damon finally took the stage, Kimmel had already instructed the speaker to introduce him as a guest of Ben Affleck and directed the orchestra to play every time Damon tried to speak.

9

Fun Facts About Matt Damon

Before fame, Matt was so broke that he had to share a joint account with his best friend, Ben Affleck. He said that the money they saved is only used for trips to New York to audition for parts. Matt then got a role in the movie Courage Under Fire. His character suffered from drug addiction problems, so he has to lose weight to portray the position accurately. He risked his life and went on an extreme self-prescribed diet and routine to lose 50 pounds in just 100 days. His way includes a 13-mile run every day and an all-chicken diet. It's incredible how much work and dedication he put into only a few minutes of the scene. The doctors told him that what he did was extremely dangerous to his health, although that role paved his success. Also, Matt has an interest in poker, in which he has competed in quite a few World Series of Poker (WSOP) events, including the main event in 2010.

10

How The World Sees Matt Damon

Matt Damon has a worldwide viewpoint that extends beyond Hollywood. When he was in his teens, he started traveling outside the USA, where he saw the reality of the world. He said that's when he realized the world was much bigger than his hometown. During one of his shoots, he spent some time with families in Africa. That experience made him see poverty and hunger in Africa, so he founded H2O Africa to bring awareness to the situation. He provided water to families in need in the said continent. He soon realized that he needed to extend his help to Africa and the whole world. Luckily, he teamed up with Gary White, a water and sanitary expert, and created water.org in 2009. They traveled the world to learn more about the issue and improve their way of helping. Matt has helped millions of lives in 13 different countries through safe water. Zenny, from the Philippines, is one of the people who received help from Water.org. She was so happy when she got a small loan from their local bank to access a water connection and now pays less than 5 percent of their monthly income on water bills. Matt wanted to empower more people to help break the cycle of poverty. He is viewed as a highly creative philanthropist.

Matt Damon is one of the few Hollywood stars to turn down most of the offered ad endorsements, although he made an exception in 2013 when he became one of the brand ambassadors for the Nespresso campaign. He agreed to work with Nespresso because he worked with people he trusts, including his co-star George Clooney, which pays enormously. He reportedly earned 3 million dollars for a 20-second scene. Matt also teamed up and endorsed a Belgium beer brand by Stella Artois. He has been helping people worldwide with clean water, and one of Stella Artois' campaigns is to donate 6.25 dollars to Matt's organization, Water.org, for every glass that has been bought. Water.org and Stella have been able to supply 800,000 people with clean water for five years. Their aim for 2020 is to reach out to 3.5 million people. Matt has also been very vocal about his political views and made a political endorsement in 2016 for Hilary Clinton.

Matt has always been engaged in ball games, especially baseball, as he is a huge Boston Red Sox fan. He used to play baseball with his friend Affleck and other ball games with his father and siblings every Sunday. Damon is a big family guy; he makes sure he spends quality time with his family despite his busy schedule. He is also an active member of the foundation ONEXONE, which aims to improve the lives of struggling children around the world. He is also promoting and taking part in activities aimed at saving the Earth. Matt also has never been shy of his political views. He is a democrat, supports Hillary Clinton, and often engages in discussions about public policy. He was once asked what his favorite cuisine is in an interview, and he responded with "Pizza."

Damon didn't grow up with great privileges. His childhood is what inspired him to make a change, and that is why he is doing everything he can through his influence to raise awareness and help people in need. He would often go to different places, visit other programs, and study their situation to understand the issue and help better. He says that when you start engaging in cases, you will begin to see a solution, and progress is being made. Matt is a highly creative philanthropist, and in his travels, he noticed that water is one of the main issues in extreme poverty, and billions of people do not have access to it. He teamed up with Gary White to launch Water.org in 2009, a charity that provides clean water for drinking and sanitation to people living in poverty around the world. Through his organization, Matt has helped over 31 million people worldwide gain access to clean water. He believes that access to water is access to a lot more in life. Aside from Water.org, he also founded H2O Africa, which brings awareness about the water crisis in Africa. He also founded Not On Our Watch together with George Clooney, Brad Pitt, Don Cheadle, and Jerry Weintraub, aiming to end mass atrocities. He supports the ONE Campaign against AIDS and poverty in third-world countries. He is also the brand ambassador of ONEXONE, which seeks to improve children's lives. Matt has over 37 charities and 30 causes, including abuse, AIDS, climate change, and more.

More than 31 million people in 13 different countries in Asia, Africa, and Latin America have received help from

Matt's organization since 2009. They give out small and affordable loans to people who need access to clean water and sanitation. His passion for ending poverty has made a lot of positive impacts on the world, and he will continue giving out help until he can.

11

Resources:

Https://abcnews.go.com/Entertainment/Oscars/matt-damon-stars/story?id=9957289#:~:text=Damon's%20first%20foray%20into%20acting,friends%20since%20the%20third%20grade.

https://www.britannica.com/biography/Matt-Damon

https://www.biography.com/actor/matt-damon

https://www.reuters.com/article/us-sexy-idUSN1418340720071114

https://www.theguardian.com/lifeandstyle/2012/mar/17/matt-damon-family-values

https://www.legacy.com/funeral-homes/obituaries/name/kent-damon-obituary?pid=187814219&v=batesville&view=guestbook

https://www.americanswhotellthetruth.org/portraits/nancy-carlsson-paige

https://www.ranker.com/list/matt-damon_s-loves-and-hookups/celebrityhookups

https://www.cheatsheet.com/entertainment/matt-damon-once-lost-50-pounds-in-100-days-for-a-role.html/

https://time.com/4473441/jimmy-kimmel-matt-damon-feud-history-timeline/

https://www.nickiswift.com/96293/untold-truth-matt-damon-ben-afflecks-friendship/

https://www.celebinvestigator.com/matt-damon/

https://www.cnbc.com/2019/02/01/wef-2019-matt-damon-on-water-charity-work.html

https://water.org/our-impact/all-stories/zeny/

12

Photo Credits

Printed in Great Britain
by Amazon